There are some mothers in this world who leave their children behind, while they are growing, for various reasons, some of which include death, divorce, crime or career. It is my express wish that this book be a hug to all those mothers and children during their difficult time of separation. To all of you, I offer my love and support. Nothing is ever permanent.

— Jen

For my daughter, Kylara.

I love you an infinity infinities. . . . .

Why did you go away Mama,
and leave me behind?

There is work I must do alone,
my love, without you by my side.

Why did you leave and travel off
so far away I couldn't see?

I had to discover a home for myself,
a place where I could be.

How long will you stay away from me —
your kisses out of reach?

Until it is time once again,
when we may each other teach.

I have not left you behind, dearest one.

I am in your heart each breath you breathe.

I am in your eyes each time you close them.

Close them now and picture me.

We will meet again when lessons have been learned, and wisdom has been achieved.

Remember sweet pea that you are, and always will be, a special part of me.

Where are you now Mama?

Please tell me.

I have a need to know.

Around the world, walking the earth, where the oceans ebb and flow.

What do you see Mama, while
you are away out there?

I see dreams growing big and strong,
coming true everywhere.

What do you feel Mama in all those places you go?

I feel love, joy and happiness from
each and every soul.

Mama I want to go with you.

Can I go along too?

No my child, this is a journey for Mama
alone and not for you.

But.........

Be patient my little peanut.

Grow strong, and curious and free.

When it is time, and we are ready, the Universe will give you back to me.

Then together we will visit the earth,
just you and me.

And see the love, joy and happiness
of what WE are meant to be.

www.ingramcontent.com/pod-product-compliance
Lightning Source LLC
Chambersburg PA
CBHW041241040426
42445CB00004B/110